Healthy Love | Toxic Love

HEALTHY LOVE | TOXIC LOVE

BY LUNA SINCLAIR

Healthy Love | Toxic Love by Luna Sinclair

ISBN: 9780645545579

Published by Luna Sinclair

To the one who taught me what love isn't.
You led me to the one who showed me what love is.

Here I compile confessions and lessons learned in love that harms and love that heals. It is my endeavour to be as vulnerable as possible in hopes that my transparency will help you to spot the difference in your own experience.

To those stuck in toxicity, please know that it is okay if you are not yet ready to do something about it, but I sincerely wish for you to one day receive the infinite affection you deserve. Within these pages, you will find a safe place to land.

confessions of a

healthy love

you used your finger
to trace
'I love you'
on my back

even though
the ink was invisible
it felt more permanent
than any other confession

I don't want to see where things go
I want to build something intentional

this time
I won't confuse
inconsistency
with potential

all I will ever want
is Sunday mornings
with you

blankets strewn about
languid eyelids

a warm place to return to

you remind me
that soft love exists

I'm sick of matching
other people's energy

this time
you match mine
and see how you grow

if you keep saying 'forever'
maybe one day
I will believe it

it should not have been
a revelation
that a relationship
can be peaceful

but before you
I only knew chaos

all I have ever wanted
is someone
who wants to
work at love together

you are all I have ever wanted

no wonder I never knew
where home was

I hadn't met you yet

it is not codependent
to be moved by
your love's experience

to be sad when they are
to be happy for their happiness

this is empathy
and partnership
this is connection

finally I understand
that love is not
just the absence of pain

you took my baggage
and made it lighter

you saw me
beyond the scars
others had left

I breathe easily
knowing
I am not a burden to you

I must try
not to sabotage
what we have

I think this time it's real

I clung to the identity
of being the one
who always
'loves harder'

but when you met me
with the same depth
I was challenged to find
new ways of defining myself

now I have space
to be more than simply
what I can give to others

you know me
in ways
I do not
know myself

I want you
to hold my hand
with joy

I want you
to show me off
to speak of me highly
when I'm not around

I want to be
someone
you can be proud of

can we stay in this bliss?
I promise this time
I won't take it for granted

the parts of you
I dislike
are the parts of me
I have disowned

the parts of me
I make peace with
are the parts of you
I learn to accept

when I love you
with a loose grip
you have space
to come back to me

I will stay when it's scary
I will stay when it's hard
I will stay when we don't see eye-to-eye
I will stay when it means I have to grow

this time it is worth staying

what if this time
I don't brace for the worst?
what if this time I envision the best?

with you
I can be expansive
I can take up space
and use my voice

with you
I stopped shrinking
stopped settling for less
than the bare minimum

how could I be so lucky
to find a best friend
in the one I love?

this time I didn't
stop doing
what I love

this time I didn't
neglect my needs

this time I continued
to prioritise my self-care

this time I held
tightly to my identity
beyond who I am in partnership

your warmth
is enough to get through
the coldest winters

I want to be here for you
in all the ways
no one was here for me

you showed me kindness
and I mistook it for danger

you showed me kindness
and I mistook it for boredom

you showed me kindness
and I'm beginning
to believe it

I know now
that even the best love
will trigger you

even the healthiest partner
will unintentionally bring up
your traumas

I know that if I must face my shadows
I wouldn't want to do so
with anyone but you

sometimes I struggle to see
what you see in me
but that doesn't mean
it's not there

I never wanted
to move slowly
before you
but now
I want to relish
every moment

now I want to
take my time
loving you

we have all the time in the world

you taught me that
the kindest thing
I can do for you
is to look after me

you weren't put here to save me
I cannot defer my healing to you
nor will I be as selfish
as to expect you
to carry me through my challenges

you are here to hold my hand
while I save myself
you are here to celebrate
my development alongside me
while I clap for yours

we are responsible to ourselves
to become better for each other

Healthy Love | Toxic Love

if you let me
I will show you
how gentle touch can be

together we cultivate
a childlike joy

we are hide and seek
and blowing bubbles
we are curiosity
and tree houses
we are magnifying glasses
held to burning leaves

you set me on fire
with your uninhibited innocence

they say the honeymoon phase ends
but I'm still waiting

to be treated
not just as a lover
but a human
unowned, raw and free
that is what you have gifted me

I don't tell you often enough
how grateful I am for you

I could write books and songs
and remind you every day
and it would still fail to capture
the extent of my gratitude

you manage to see
beyond what I show
and for that I will always love you

You have held a mirror
up to me in all my glory
and I am finally
beginning to like what I see

I hoped that real love would be sunshine and stress-free at all times. I now know that healthy love means conflict. Healthy love means getting uncomfortable at times, while being supported in a safe environment. Healthy love means challenging yourself and each other.

Healthy love has its moments of stress and hard work, but the growth it catalyses is invaluable.

we have our differences
but our love is the same

show me where it hurts
I'll place my hand over it

tell me about your fears
I'll shine a light in the dark for you

show me all of you
I will gaze upon you with tender eyes

can I borrow some of your faith in us?
mine has never led me far

I don't want your perfection
I want your effort

what magic
must you possess
to make me feel
so peaceful and passionate
all at once

you pour
the sweetest contradictions
into me

you are the first person
whose interest in me
I am not waiting to fade

you came to me
with peace built in

your presence
puts me at such ease
I could sleep for days

finally I have found
a place to rest

even if we met earlier
I would still never have
enough time with you

Healthy Love | Toxic Love

love is red roses and chocolates
but it's also taking the middle seat
on a red eye flight
so they get the aisle

it's swallowing your pride
and apologising

it's being ready to hear all your flaws
without defensiveness

the beauty of our love is that
you leave me with more answers
than questions

you are sunshine when there is none

it's just you and I
and this beautiful little world
we're creating

toxic love

if I don't reach out first
will I ever hear from you again?

no one with good intentions
has to tell you
they're 'not like the others'

my unhealed self
kept finding new ways
to recreate my hurt
and you were all too happy
to step up to the plate

never again
will I settle
for someone
who isn't sure about me

instead of questioning
why I wasn't good enough
maybe I should be questioning
why you couldn't see my value

Healthy Love | Toxic Love

I keep holding back my love
as if it's inconvenient
as if my care is not a privilege

when it's the wrong love:

1. You keep googling if their behaviour is normal
2. You're constantly distracting yourself from how bad you feel
3. You change your appearance often hoping they'll notice
4. You never know where you really stand
5. Their love changes day to day
6. You fear that if you tell them how you feel, it will destroy things

communication only works
if you're willing to listen

isn't it ironic
when I lost you
I thought
I'd never be happy again

as if I was happy with you
in the first place

it felt like it was ending
from the very beginning

I refuse to take on shame
that isn't mine

I refuse to dehumanize myself
the way you dehumanized me

waiting for you
didn't bring you back
it just kept me
from moving forward

can we go back to a time
where dating meant something

can we go back to a time
before 'situationships'
left us chronically detached

can we go back to a time
when talking stages
led to something real

can we go back to a time
before ghosting and breadcrumbing
became a regular part of my vocabulary

playing games didn't bring us closer
they pushed me further from myself

I snap a rubber band on my wrist
when I think of you
as if our memories
don't sting enough

I make excuses
for people
I would never make
for myself

you made me believe
I was broken
that something
was wrong with me

you turned my feelings
into problems

labeled me too emotional
too much
too clingy
too human

I wish I could go home
I wish I knew where home was

I'm sick of 'it's complicated'
it doesn't have to be

give me all-in
give me long-lasting
please just make it simple

our love left bruises
in places
I still haven't discovered

why must I look for reasons to stay?
why can't you look for actions to keep
me?

Healthy Love | Toxic Love

second choice
　　would have been
　　　　a step up
　　　　　from where
　　　　　　you kept me

did I make all this up?
was it all in my head?

or did you manipulate me
into believing in something
that never was real

you left the door open
not out of love
but convenience

the closure was leaving
your messages unread

the closure was reclaiming
everything I loved
that you shamed me for

the closure was forgetting
your middle name
and not reaching out on birthdays

sometimes I wonder
if you loved me
just to pass the time

the manipulation
was so subtle
I didn't realise
how cunningly
I was being shaped
into someone
I no longer recognised

you told me you would never hurt me
while doing the opposite

I'm still waiting
for your promises
to come true

I wonder how many lifetimes
it would take before they did

my intuition knew
you weren't good for me
far before my mind ever did

I wish loving me
wasn't on your list of chores

if I hide everything
that reminds me of you
can I hide from heartbreak too?

I am tired of decoding messages
reading between lines

love me clearly or leave

never again will I give away my power
not everyone deserves a piece

all I want
is a love
that won't make me
miss the beginning

all I want
is a love
with a future
not just a past

why does it hurt so much
to get over someone
who only ever brought you pain?

I don't give up on people easily
maybe that's why I stayed too long

how many pieces of myself
will I have to give away
before I am enough for you?

and now
we're strangers
again

but I can never
get back
the person I was
before you

Healthy Love | Toxic Love

I used to be surprised
when you let me down

now I expect it

I don't want
to harden my heart
just because
you don't know
how to soften yours

how small must I be
before I am acceptable to you?

the butterflies you gave me
weren't a sign of love
but a sign I didn't feel safe

when I tried to act like you
I stopped caring for me too

I'm over starting sentences
with 'sorry'
as if my existence
is inconvenient

people can change
but you don't have to
wait around
for them to get there

I had to keep looking
for signs from the universe
when reality
was too hard to face

who do I run to
if the person who is my comfort
is the person causing my pain?

I had to convince myself
that you were just tired
just having a bad day
just quiet

I couldn't come to terms
with the fact that you
just didn't

care

you swore
you would never
be good enough for me

but you could have at least tried

thank you for showing me
what I won't tolerate in future

thank you for showing me
that I deserved better

thank you for showing me
the warning signs to look out for

things were never as good
with you
as my mind painted them to be

is it too much to ask
for one night's rest
on a pillow that isn't
tear-stained

why must I keep
looking for flaws
within myself
when someone else
lets me down?

you refused to evolve
so I evolved for us both

am I a bad judge of character
or are you a good liar?

you knew I was miserable
and yet you were surprised
when I did something about it

how foolish to think
I would allow you
to paint my days grey

you saved your worst moments
for me in private

you watched me fall apart
and you said nothing

you watched me curl up in pain
and you turned away

you watched me
become a shell of myself
and you took pride
in how hollow you could make me

there was always a little bit of truth
in the painful jokes you told

Healthy Love | Toxic Love

it stings initially
but just wait for the relief
of no longer having to accomodate
for someone
who is so clearly uninterested
in returning the favour

I don't know what the reason is for this
but I know in the end
it will be for the best

no matter where I am now
no matter what you tell me
I will make something of myself

our forever was cut short
and only later
would I learn
what a blessing
this would one day be

Healthy Love | Toxic Love

Thank you for opening your heart to receive mine. I am eternally grateful for your immense capacity for vulnerability. Here's to all of us who are still brave enough to love.

If you enjoyed Healthy Love | Toxic Love please consider leaving a review on Amazon.

Healthy Love | Toxic Love